Final Years of
Isle of Wight Steam

Tony Molyneaux and Kevin Robertson

Ian Allan PUBLISHING

Front cover: Recorded in July 1965, Class O2 0-4-4 tank No W27 *Merstone* leaves Sandown on the 4.48pm departure to Ventnor. The 'O2s' were the staple motive power in the final years of Isle of Wight steam, no fewer than 23 members of the class having been transferred from the mainland between 1925 and 1949. *Tony Molyneaux*

Back cover: On what would appear to be a windy day No W27 *Merstone* is blowing off steam at Sandown as it waits to head north for Brading and Ryde on 31 August 1963. Note the mother who has brought her children to watch the train depart — or perhaps it was Dad who was the persuading influence. *Tony Molyneaux*

Title page: A wonderful view of a 'fast' service from Ryde Pier Head to Ventnor, headed by No W18 *Ningwood* and formed of alternate green-and red-liveried stock, passing non-stop through Ryde St Johns on 20 June 1959. The train also omitted stops at Ryde Esplanade and Sandown. To the right is the exterior of the locomotive works; the running shed was on the opposite side of the line. Note also, at the far end of St Johns Hill road bridge, the tall starting signal; a co-acting arm was provided which was seen in an earlier view. The need to co-ordinate the remainder of the service meant that in BR days limited-stop operation was confined to three trains a day, which hardly compared with the position in 1897, when trains ran non-stop from Ryde to Ventnor and took just 20min for the entire journey! The earliest record of a non-stop service was as far back as 1891, when what was known locally as the 'Invalid Express', run for the benefit of those wishing to take the air. It survived in the timetables until 1909. *John Bailey*

Right: A green survivor recorded in the 1970s. *Ian Whitmarsh*

Bibliography

A Locomotive History of Railways on the Isle of Wight, D. L. Bradley (Railway Correspondence & Travel Society, 1982)
Branch Lines to Newport, Vic Mitchell and Keith Smith (Middleton Press, 1985)
Isle of Wight Central Railway, R. J. Maycock and R. Silsbury (Oakwood Press, 2001)
Isle of Wight Railway, R. J. Maycock and R. Silsbury (Oakwood Press, 1999)
Isle of Wight Steam Passenger Rolling Stock, R. J. Maycock and M. J. E. Reed (Oakwood Press, 1997)
Once upon a Line. Vol 1, Andrew Britton (OPC, 1983)
Rails in the Isle of Wight, P. C. Allen and A. B. McCloud (George Allen & Unwin, 1967)
Return to Ryde by Steam, Andrew Britton (Medina Books, 2005)
Ryde by Steam. Volume 1, Andrew Britton (Medina Books, 2004)
South Coast Railways: Ryde to Ventnor, Vic Mitchell and Keith Smith (Middleton Press, 1985)
The Signalling of the Isle of Wight Railways (Signalling Record Society, 1993)

First published 2007

ISBN (10) 0 7110 3241 6
ISBN (13) 978 0 7110 3241 5

Published by Ian Allan Publishing

an imprint of Ian Allan Publishing Ltd, Hersham, Surrey, KT12 4RG
Printed in England by Ian Allan Printing Ltd, Hersham, Surrey, KT12 4RG

Code: 0705/B1

Visit the Ian Allan Publishing website at www.ianallanpublishing.com

Introduction

Almost a microcosm of Victorian England, the Isle of Wight became a veritable Mecca for steam enthusiasts in the years leading up to the end of 1966; here, still, were branch-line trains hauled by Victorian steam locomotives pulling coaches of which some dated back to the Edwardian era. It was the last place where this could be witnessed, the 'blue' era associated with the general railway modernisation of the 1960s being — for the moment, at least — kept at bay.

It has been claimed that the island, just 30 miles wide by 15 miles deep, could accommodate the world's entire population standing shoulder to shoulder. It may even be questioned as to who on earth might promulgate such a useless fact, but I guess it could be someone who has perhaps witnessed the Isle of Wight at peak holiday time, when it may have

appeared as if a fair proportion of the world had indeed congregated in such a small area. Fortunately though the Isle of Wight is relatively well anchored and is thus unlikely to sink or drift away despite the influx of visitors.

The increase in population is, of course, only seasonal and affects primarily the island's east side around the coastal areas of Sandown, Shanklin and Ventnor. In the days when most visitors would arrive at Ryde as foot passengers the railway was the principal means of transport to and from the resorts, and at times on a summer Saturday, with holidaymakers both arriving and departing, the terminus at Ryde might be said to have resembled a mini Waterloo.

But the railway system did not just run south from Ryde to Ventnor. There were numerous branches, chief amongst them being that branching

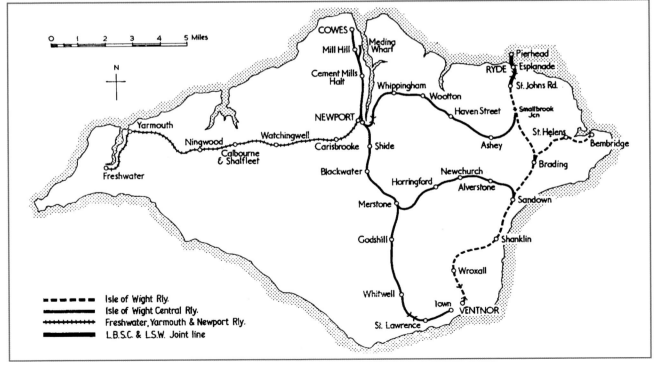

Right: The Isle of Wight railway system at its greatest extent. By the late 1950s only the Ryde–Ventnor, Ryde–Newport–Cowes lines were still open. The Newport–Yarmouth, Newport–Ventnor West and Sanddown–Merstone lines closing earlier in the decade.

off westwards at Smallbrook Junction (just south of Ryde) and heading towards Newport — the island's administrative capital — and eventually Cowes. At one time there were also routes to Bembridge, Freshwater and Ventnor West, that to the last branching off another now closed line that once connected Newport and Sandown direct. All of these succumbed early in BR days, and the routes between Ryde and Ventnor, and Ryde, Newport and Cowes were the only ones to survive to the end of steam.

Much has been written of the island's railways, foremost amongst these a superb history by Allen and McCloud, based on much personal experience. In more recent times even more detail has appeared in a comprehensive series of books by Maycock and Silsbury, whilst local anecdotes are related in Andrew Britton's wonderfully nostalgic 'Once on a Line' series, sadly now out of print. All of these have been consulted in the compilation of this volume and are acknowledged in the bibliography.

Why, then, another book? The answer is simple. A trawl through Tony Molyneaux's collection of colour slides revealed a wealth of unpublished material on the island's railways, while another Hampshire enthusiast, John Bailey, has made available his collection, which has also lain dormant for

several decades. It was an opportunity, then, not to be missed. Further material has come from Paul Bodkin, Terry Cole, Doug Hannah, Bert Moody and Bob Winkworth. To all of the above I extend my grateful thanks.

From a personal perspective also, this is an album I have long wished to have the opportunity to compile. I well recall as a youth in the 1960s visiting Cowes and hearing the loud bark of an 'O2' as it shunted its train from the station ready to allow the coaches to run back into the platform. It was sound also that was heard year after year and coincided with what seemed to be an annual day trip from Southampton. It was something that, as an impressionable youth, I took for granted; I could not have imagined that Cowes would ever be a place without a train service. Sadly we never travelled by train on the occasions of those visits; indeed, I cannot seem to recall exactly what we did do! I could hardly have imagined either that, just a few years later, work commitments would see me living for a year at West Cowes. By then the trains had gone, but although the track had been lifted the course of the railway was still evident, and many a time I found myself walking though the tunnel at Mill Hill or exploring the decaying terminus.

The route from Cowes to Newport was the penultimate steam-operated line on the island, that south from Ryde being the very last — discounting the present-day preserved section at Haven Street. Elsewhere on the island closures had been taking place in stages from the early 1950s, one example being the line from Freshwater to Newport, which closed on 21 September 1953 together with the associated intermediate stopping places of Yarmouth, Ningwood, Calbourne, Watchingwell and Carisbrooke. Here No W36 *Carisbrooke* is depicted awaiting departure from the Freshwater terminus early in BR days. Slightly unusually the locomotive is facing towards Newport. *Paul Bodkin*

But this present work is not intended to be a book of personal reminiscences from the days after closure. Instead it is, as already stated, a volume of unpublished views, mainly from the period from the late 1950s to the end of 1966. After that time British Railways decided to close the whole system for 'modernisation', after which there remained only a truncated stub between Ryde and Shanklin, operated by electric traction. Since then the surviving rump has been further 'rationalised' by the removal of everything save the most basic requirements for serving what is in effect a long siding with a passing loop over which ex-London Underground trains shuttle to and fro. Freight is a thing of the past, whilst holiday peaks of traffic are something the modern operators do not welcome or, indeed, have in place the infrastructure and rolling stock to deal with.

Steam might have survived longer on the island had the plans of the mid-1960s come to fruition. For, after the rejection of the original Beeching proposal to close the island's entire system, BR was faced with a dilemma with regard to the existing stock of locomotives and coaches. The 'O2'-class 0-4-4Ts were already of pensionable age, and the rolling stock was rapidly heading the same way, but the island's restricted loading gauge severely limited the scope for modern replacements.

In terms of motive power, thoughts of a more modern steam replacements manifested themselves with the arrival at Eastleigh in 1965 of a Standard Class 2 tank, No 84020. As it stood it was physically too tall for use on the Isle of Wight, but it had come with a view to assessing whether a cut-down version was feasible, the plan being for 10 of these locomotives to be so converted. Ultimately nothing came of the idea, but it was a bold attempt. Whether this failure was down to cost, a political desire to abandon steam altogether or other, unknown issues is not clear; possibly the difficulty of recruiting steam crews was a consideration. Information regarding potential replacement for the coaching stock appears not to have survived.

With the benefit of hindsight it is clear that, had there been a will, the continued use on the Ryde–Shanklin line of steam on special occasions, supplemented by diesel or electric traction for normal services, could well have attracted additional tourism. This argument has, of course, been used elsewhere in relation to other lines but, as far as I am aware, has never won the day.

Of course, the trippers that do still visit the island — and there are still thousands — now often bring their own cars, so it could perhaps be said that the need for public transport has diminished. But there again, four decades ago no-one could quite have foreseen the increase that would take place in vehicular traffic, to the extent that the roads can no longer cope. Indeed, a visit in the early summer of 2006 indicated the presence of several speed cameras to be totally irrelevant: due to traffic volume it was simply not possible to travel fast enough to reach — let alone exceed — the speed limit!

Unfortunately the notion of restoring the island's railways as a means of public transport can now be no more than a pipe-dream (although there is certainly a need, today's bus services being far from ideal on such congested roads); with land at a premium, much of the trackbed of the various closed lines has been converted for other uses. In one area, however, around Haven Street, on part of the former Newport line from Ryde, steam can be still be witnessed, with the preserved line a wonderful example of how things once were. It has a charm all of its own and is well worth a visit. There is even a platform connection with the 'main line' at the erstwhile Smallbrook Junction.

What follows is an exercise in pure nostalgia, enjoyed by both Tony and myself in its compilation and, I trust, also to be enjoyed by those who read it. With one exception (a favourite view of the terminus at Freshwater) I have deliberately avoided covering the routes closed early in BR days. Accordingly this album 'does what it says on the tin', serving as a record of the final years of the Ryde–Ventnor and Ryde–Cowes lines.

For those who, like me, recall Isle of Wight steam in its final years, this book (which features every member of the 'O2' class active in the 1960s) should evoke some happy memories; for others I trust it will give a flavour of an era now passed. Either way, I hope you enjoy the selection.

Kevin Robertson
Corhampton
March 2007

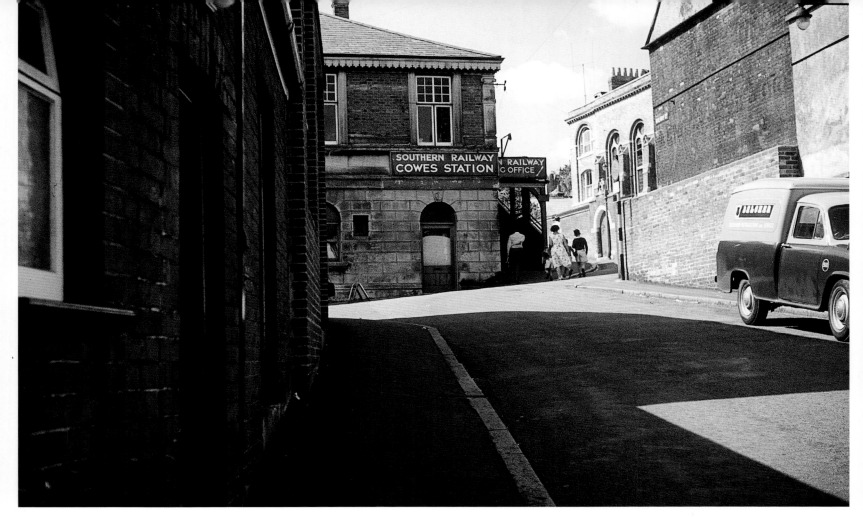

The steep approach to Cowes station from Railway Street — West Cowes, to be more accurate, as the town of East Cowes is on the opposite side of the River Medina. Holidaymakers would arrive on the island by ferry at one of four locations — to the west using the Lymington–Yarmouth service (although the island train service from the nearby station had ceased after the end of the 1953 summer service), at Cowes, where the boats from Southampton would call at both East and West Cowes, at Fishbourne, used mainly by road vehicles but where there was no adjacent rail access, and finally at Ryde. Both the Fishbourne and Ryde ferries emanated from Portsmouth. Unfortunately the geography of the town meant the station at Cowes was some distance from the ferry, hence as road competition developed the latter had a definite advantage. Recorded near the end of the 1964 summer season, on 29 August, a small group of intrepid travellers can be seen just about to enter the station. On the right is a Morris van from the Belcher's Television business, whilst the 'H'-type aerial atop the house in the distance is another reminder of those 405-line days. *Paul Bodkin*

Right: No W33 *Bembridge* stands at the buffer-stops at Cowes on Sunday 15 August 1965 with a train from Ryde, which journey took around 40 minutes inclusive of six intermediate stops. This locomotive was one of four sent to the island in May 1936 and with No W14 would survive until the end of steam in December 1966. On the extreme right the brick building with flat concrete roof could well be a wartime air-raid shelter. The footbridge from which this scene was recorded secured a public right of way and was irrelevant to railway operation, but it nevertheless provided a useful vantage-point for photographers! *John Bailey*

Right: Captured again at the same location (but by a different photographer and on a different occasion), No W33 *Bembridge* has run around its train and is gently rolling forward to couple up before departing for Newport and Ryde. Granville Road bridge is in the background. Ten minutes was the normal allowance to turn a 'down' service into an 'up' service ready to depart, the usual procedure being for the locomotive of an arriving train to push its stock back beyond the engine-release crossover, after which it would run around, and the coaches would be 'gravity shunted' back into the same platform. Other than once a day mid-morning and on busy summer Saturdays it was rare for passenger services to use other than Platform 1. Notice the grass in the 'four-foot', whilst the starting signal is already 'off' in anticipation of the departure. Cowes station was renowned also for its hanging flower baskets under the glazed canopy at the end of the platforms. Passenger services here ceased in February 1966. *Terry Cole*

Two passenger trains at Cowes on Friday 7 August 1964, although there is only one locomotive visible, this being No W22 *Brading*. The wooden signalbox on the left contained a frame of 20 levers, including one spare. Token working was also in use to Newport, this having replaced tablet working in June 1958. Judging from the appearance of the staiths on the left, some coal was still being handled, although the rusty rails elsewhere suggest that other freight traffic was by now almost non-existent. *Tony Molyneaux*

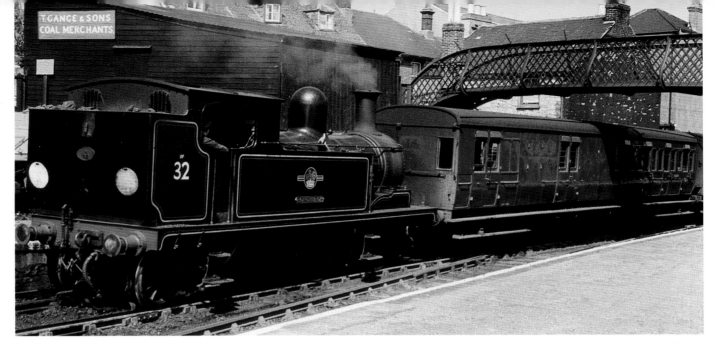

Right: A wonderfully clean No W32 *Bonchurch* awaiting departure for Newport — and Ryde, of course — on 18 April 1960. The locomotive still displays its original brass nameplate; several of these were replaced in later years by cheap metal pressings to thwart unscrupulous collectors. On the rear of the bunker is another oval brass plate with the locomotive number. *John Bailey*

Below right: Viewed from the end of the platform at Cowes sometime in the summer of 1965, No W24 *Calbourne* waits impatiently for departure time. Notice the sharp curvature, necessitating the 'Mind the Gap' warning on both platforms. Aside from the curves, departing trains were faced with a gradient of 1 in 67 commencing at the end of the platform. The yellow ground signal controlled movement across the engine-release crossover but also permitted shunting manœuvres to the end of Platform 2. Notice also the check rail, provided due to the curvature of both platforms. *Doug Hannah*

Cowes from Granville Road bridge, recorded on 18 April 1960. Unfortunately on this occasion the identity of the locomotive was not recorded, but it could well be No W32 again. The man at the end of the platform, walking towards the train, is probably the signalman, whose bicycle can be seen propped up against the inside rail of the siding on the left. Back in the late 19th century there had been a proposal and even authorisation for a tramway linking the station and pier, but it was destined never to be built. *John Bailey*

Right: No W24 *Calbourne* disturbs the peace at Cowes whilst waiting to depart on a glorious summer's evening in 1965. The mouth of the River Medina is in the background, with the town and industry of East Cowes, famed for yachting, on the far bank; a considerable quantity of expensive floating hardware is also visible. In the background can just be seen the top of a Red Funnel vessel — possibly, from the date of the photograph, one of the 'Castle' type — operating the ferry service to Southampton. *Terry Cole*

Right: The curvature of the line is well illustrated here as No W30 *Shorwell*, in charge of the 6.28pm Ryde service, climbs away from Cowes station prior to entering Mill Hill Tunnel. The houses face onto St Mary's Road, which the railway crossed by means of a low iron girder bridge. The two signals, from left to right Nos 19 and 18, home signals for Platforms 1 and 2, were located just 225yd from Cowes signalbox. No W30 had just 18 months left in service when the photograph was taken on 29 March 1964. *John Bailey*

Left: Serving the southwest of the town, Mill Hill station at Cowes dated from almost the very start of the then independent Cowes & Newport Railway. No goods facilities were ever provided, but the 404ft platform saw a heavy volume of workers during the week. Here, on 15 August 1965, we see a Cowes-bound train about to depart and enter the 208yd Mill Hill Tunnel on the final leg of its journey, Mill Hill station being just 770yd from the terminus. Note that the outline of the tunnel has been picked out in white. The pathway led up to Newport Road, the wooden station buildings being behind the camera. *John Bailey*

Above: Almost journey's end for No W31 *Chale*, waiting to leave Mill Hill for the final hop to Cowes in the summer of 1965. The building here dated from 1880 and was the second station on the site, the original having been destroyed by fire after standing for only nine years. The houses on the opposite side of the line are fronting Gordon Road. *Terry Cole*

Left: Beyond Mill Hill in the direction of Newport was first of all Smithard's Crossing and then a small siding for the gasworks; after this was Medina Wharf, located on the river of the same name, which in its flow north effectively splits Cowes into an East and West side, the two being linked by a chain ferry. Medina Wharf, located one mile from Cowes, was also the location where most of the later stock transfers of locomotives and rolling stock, having arrived from Southampton, were unloaded by floating crane. The cost was kept to a minimum as the Southern Railway also owned the docks and the crane! The principal traffic dealt with here was coal inwards, and Island produce sent outwards, although in both cases the goods themselves were trans-shipped and not the wagons. Indeed, so great was this traffic that prior to 1939 there were over 600 goods wagons operating the island's rail system, of which 500 were 'opens'. This is a general view of the wharf itself from the main line on 7 May 1960. No W27 *Merstone* is doing the shunting. *John Bailey*

Below left: No W27 again, in course of shunting the now rather overgrown 620ft 'No 1 road'. The 1-in-60 gradient from the wharf meant that coal trains were sometimes brought up a few wagons at a time. Traditionally coal trains would be handled by one of the island's four 'E1' 0-6-0T locomotives, although at the time the photograph was taken (7 May 1960) just one, No W4, was left in service. No W27 would itself be one of the island's last locomotives, remaining in service until December 1966. *John Bailey*

Right: Merstone has now brought its train up the 1-in-60 gradient from the sidings onto what was referred to as simply the 'right-hand road', the connection to the main line being behind the camera. Even in the 1960s there were still two coal trains daily from here to Newport to feed the demand of the local merchants, whilst locomotive coal for Ryde depot also arrived here and was worked 'as required'. For workers at the wharf a short timber platform was provided on the main line, although this did not appear in the public timetable. *John Bailey*

Already recorded earlier the same day – 7 May 1960 – at Medina Wharf, No W27 is seen running through Newport on its way to Ryde; the train is gaining the single line with the down platform loop visible. Prior to 1958 a second single line, to Merstone and Ventnor West, diverged here, although the passenger service on this route had ceased a few years earlier; subsequently the trackwork and signalling at this end of Newport station were rationalised, and where previously a scissors crossover once existed there was now just a single turnout at the end of the loop. Some evidence of past times can be gauged from the bracket signal visible above the train and where there is now only a single post in place. This type of goods traffic continued on the Newport–Cowes line for a time after passenger services ceased serving not just Medina Wharf but also the nearly Cement Mills siding. *John Bailey*

Attached to a pair of four-wheeled SR utility vans, an absolutely filthy No W27 *Merstone* waits in what had been the Freshwater bay at Newport in 1965; trains using the Freshwater line had had to perform a reversal when arriving at or departing Newport. At its peak the island's rail network boasted a route mileage of just over 55 miles together with 36 stations. *Terry Cole*

Above: A stunningly clean No W14 *Fishbourne* about to leave Newport on 7 May 1960 with a train for Ryde, the first coach of which can be identified as Brake Third No S4144, originally part of four-coach set No 488. Immediately ahead is the famous Medina drawbridge, whilst beyond is Newport Viaduct; the Ryde line curves away to the left, while the by-now derelict viaduct on the erstwhile route to Merstone can be discerned on the right. Prior to 1958 Newport South signalbox had stood on the right, just before the viaduct; in that year, to avoid a long walk for the signalman and crews when required to obtain a token to proceed towards Haven Street, an auxiliary token instrument was installed at the south end of the station. *John Bailey*

Right: No W31 *Chale* on the viaduct at Newport, bound for Haven Street and Ryde. At the time this locomotive was carrying a Drummond boiler, identifiable through having the safety valves atop the dome rather than the firebox, as was the case with the Adams boiler. *Terry Cole*

Left: The next two stations on the route towards Smallbrook Junction and Ryde — Whippingham and Wootton — both closed in 1953, following which Haven Street was the first stopping-place after Newport, 4 miles 32 chains from Newport South and approximately the same distance from Smallbrook. Post 1956, following the demolition of the signalbox at Whippingham, this was also the first token-point after Newport, meaning the passing loop here was often busy. In this view, recorded on 1 August 1960, No W28 *Ashey* is entering the station on a glorious summer's evening in charge of the 6.30pm Ryde–Cowes service, scheduled to cross here with the 6.24pm Cowes–Ryde. Two years later, in 1962, this locomotive would receive the side tanks from the withdrawn No W25, it being the practice at Ryde Works to utilise parts from whatever source to keep the remaining stock in service. *John Bailey*

Above right: Moving ahead a few years, to 5 August 1964, we find No W17 *Seaview* waiting at the looped platform at Haven Street with the 12.48pm (12.24pm ex Cowes) to Ryde. The fireman will have a slight breather here, as the train is awaiting the arrival of the 12.30pm from Ryde. Singly the 'O2'-class locomotives were limited to a maximum load of 187 tons for passenger trains on the Cowes line and 155-160 tons (dependent upon the weather) on the Ventnor line. The two discs at the bottom of the bunker represent the correct headcode for services in either direction between Ryde and Cowes. *Tony Molyneaux*

Right: A few moments later No W20 *Shanklin* arrives from the opposite direction and with the signalman ready to exchange tokens — unusually the old-style leather tablet pouch is still being used. Movement between the platforms here was by means of a board crossing visible under the locomotive, road access to the station being via a forecourt out of shot to the right. *Tony Molyneaux*

Above: The 1926-built station building at Haven Street, recorded from a train leaving for Ryde on Saturday 25 July 1964. For many years Haven Street was the recipient of a wooden seat, awarded to the best-kept station on the island; no doubt this was due to the neat garden display, part of which is just visible in the foreground. *John Bailey*

Right: Venturing eastwards we reach the station at Ashey, where No W26 *Whitwell* was recorded in charge of an evening service for Cowes in September 1965. Ashey station was reduced in status to that of an unstaffed halt in 1953, whilst movement of the clay subsoil here caused the running line to be slewed south in 1961 to the position formerly occupied by the down loop. By this time also passenger traffic was extremely limited — a far cry from decades past, when as many as 3,000 racegoers would arrive for the twice-yearly Ashey horse-race meeting. The station building, somewhat ornate even for years past, was reputedly provided at the behest of the local landowner. Despite its by-now derelict appearance it was subsequently resurrected as a private dwelling. *Terry Cole*

Left: Summer at Smallbrook Junction, the point of divergence (or convergence, dependent upon one's perspective) of the Cowes and Ventnor lines. The ground-level timber signalbox controlling movements here was situated in the 'V' of the junction and contained a frame of 20 levers, including five spares. Recorded on 9 June 1962, No W22 *Brading* has charge of a Cowes-line service and is hauling one of the regular three-coach loads. In the background can be seen the bracket holding the inner home signals, of which No 17 is in the 'off' position for the train. Notice the concrete posts sunk at intervals into the 'four-foot'; these were placed where it was suspected the track might be deviating from its original alignment, the distance between the running rails and the metal point on top of the concrete being measured at regular intervals thereafter so as to identify any 'creep' that might have taken place. *John Bailey*

Above right: Viewed from a similar vantage-point on Saturday 3 July 1965, No W17 *Seaview*, displaying duty board No 8, takes the Cowes line. The duty boards were an adjunct to the headcode discs and assisted in identifying the actual service — in this case the 3.45pm Saturday service from Ryde — as well as the route to be taken. No W17 also shows signs of an earlier build-up of cinders within the smokebox, which has caused the paint to peel off the lower part of the door. *Tony Molyneaux*

Right: Recorded from the opposite side, No W24 *Calbourne* (nowadays the solitary preserved example of the 'O2' class) prepares to join the double-line section to Ryde on 3 July 1965. Aside from two possibly unofficial visitors to the signalbox (the island lines were invariably friendly and accommodating to *bona fide* visitors), a number of what appear to be watering containers can be seen at the foot of the signalbox steps. *Tony Molyneaux*

No book on Isle of Wight steam would be complete without a view of the ferry services from the mainland — even if the Solent has long been reputed to be, mile-for-mile (nautical, of course!), the most expensive stretch of water to cross in the world. This is PS *Ryde*, approaching Ryde Pier Head with what appears to be a goodly complement of trippers. Built in 1937, with a displacement of 603 tons and capable of carrying no fewer than 1,011 passengers at a maximum speed of 14 knots, this vessel survived in service until 1969 and remains extant, although derelict as PS *Ryde Queen*. *Paul Bodkin*

The classic view of the train on the pier, with No W31 *Chale* about to head the short distance towards Esplanade with a Ventnor train. In the foreground (left) are the rails of the tramway, whilst on the right the stop signal (No 25 in the Ryde Pier Head signalbox, seen on the left) has an electric route indicator attached to inform the crew as to which of the four platforms they will be routed into. *Doug Hannah*

Left: No W22 *Brading* receiving attention from the crew prior to departure from Ryde in the summer of 1964. Indeed, the footplateman could well be in the process of giving the Westinghouse pump a clout with a spanner, a strictly unofficial but usually quite successful method of cajoling this vital component into functioning correctly. The locomotive is standing at the south end of the 388ft Platform 1 at the Pier Head, the single headcode disc indicating that it was about to work an all-stations service to Ventnor. This particular platform was added in 1933 but was subsequently removed in connection with electrification. *Chris Webb*

Right: A summer's evening *c*1965, with No W31 *Chale* waiting to depart from Platform 3 at Ryde Pier Head. Just visible to the right is the electric tramway linking Pier Head and Esplanade. In the background is the town of Ryde itself, whilst nearer to the camera is the 28-lever timber-framed signalbox. *Bob Winkworth*

S 4153

Load 2½ Tons.

31

Left: Running parallel with the railway between Ryde Pier Head and Ryde Esplanade was the 700yd pier tramway, which had been operated by the railway company for many years. Its chief purpose was to provide additional capacity for travellers arriving by ferry and intending to travel only as far as Ryde, such an influx being otherwise likely to swamp the railway service. The tramway was in operation for more than 100 years, for most of that time using electricity, although both equine and steam power had periods of use in earlier times. Recorded in April 1969 at the Esplanade end of the tramway, the service outlived the steam railway by just over two years, operating for the last time in January 1969. *Doug Hannah*

Above: On 5 August 1964 — clearly a warm day — No W17 *Seaview* prepares to set off from Ryde Esplanade on the last (32-chain, or 704yd) leg of its journey to Ryde Pier Head. The number of pedestrians walking in the opposite direction, scorning both tramway and railway in favour of a 'constitutional', suggests a boat has just arrived. *Tony Molyneaux*

Above: At the opposite end of the Esplanade station No W17 *Seaview* blows off steam prior to departing with the 3.29pm Ventnor service on 3 August 1964. Again, the characteristic sharp curves so typical of the island lines are apparent, the brick- and timber-built station here fronting a curve of no less than 9-chain (198yd) radius. *Tony Molyneaux*

Right: Signs of maintenance in the form of paint pots and men in between the tramway tracks on 5 August 1964. No W26 *Whitwell* is reported by the photographer as being on a Cowes train yet displays a 'Newport–Ventnor West' headcode. The signals here were controlled from the Pier Head signalbox, and track circuiting was provided on both platform lines, hence the presence of the telltale 'diamond' on the post. *Tony Molyneaux*

Above: No W27 *Merstone* descends the steep (1-in-30) gradient and slightly wider-radius (10-chain) curve from Ryde Esplanade station towards Ryde Tunnel. The locomotive is in charge of a Ventnor 'fast' formed of six vehicles. This was the summer of 1964; note the wonderful collection of contemporary motor coaches on the right. *Terry Cole*

Right: Entering the 391yd Ryde Tunnel on a southbound train on 20 June 1959. The stone plaque between the arches gives the date of building, whilst passing atop the tunnel is The Esplanade. Despite the twin-arched approach the tunnel itself was a single bore and in periods of continuous wet weather had been known to flood. Above the tunnel the sense of nostalgia is perpetuated by the period road sign, coach-built perambulator and a coach, possibly a Bedford. *John Bailey*

Left: An unidentified member of the 'O2' class on the approach to Ryde St Johns with a Ventnor-line train in August 1964. To the right is the start of the down loop, whilst also visible is the banner repeater for down trains, which advised the crew of the position of the starting signal at the end of the platform. *Doug Hannah*

Above: Parcels duty for No W24 *Calbourne*, posed outside the signalbox at Ryde St Johns in May 1966. In terms of the number of levers (40) Ryde St Johns signalbox, originally located at Waterloo East, was the largest on the island. The locomotive is in the final livery for the class in British Railways days, plain unlined black, which

bland style, devoid of nameplates, was described by D. L. Bradley in *A Locomotive History of Railways on the Isle of Wight* (RCTS, 1982) as 'the final indignity'. The locomotive is attached to passenger guard's van No S1015, a former SECR passenger coach converted in December 1956; the train is probably the regular Shanklin–Ryde parcels service. St Johns was the largest of the three stations at Ryde and was where the island's locomotive and carriage workshops were located, together with the running shed. (Another locomotive shed at Newport had closed in November 1957.) In the background is No W31 *Chale*. *Bob Winkworth*

Above: South of St Johns trains were faced with an initial climb of 1 in 220 followed by further uphill gradients to Smallbrook Junction and beyond on both the Cowes and Ventnor lines. This undated photograph shows No W14 *Fishbourne* about to depart. The wheel in the foreground (right) controlled the supply of water to the platform column, while the elevated disc signals were used to control shunting. *Paul Bodkin*

Right: Another view of No W14 at Ryde St Johns, this time in charge of the 11.33am departure for Ventnor on 5 August 1964. Notice the protective cover placed over the Westinghouse pump; not all the locomotives appeared to have this, although No W17 certainly did. The flexible hose for the steam-heat connection is missing but would not have been needed at this time of year anyway. The wall on the opposite platform provides a good example of the Southern Railway's use of concrete. *Tony Molyneaux*

Left: A trio of 'O2s' — two of which are recorded as Nos W16 and W14, though the order is unknown — photographed on 5 August 1964 outside Ryde St Johns locomotive shed, which stood on the west side of the station. Nos W16 and W14 both arrived on the island in May 1936 and would survive until the end of steam. *Tony Molyneaux*

Above: Taken in May 1966, this photograph clearly shows the front of the two-road locomotive shed, while to the left is the coal road; coaling appears to have been a muscle-powered activity. Five locomotives — Nos W31, W29, W26, W16, and W33 — are visible. Interestingly No W29 was the only one of the Isle of Wight locomotives ever to return to the mainland after conversion at Eastleigh; this was in 1947, when it went back for overhaul, after which it returned to end its days on the island. *Bob Winkworth*

Right: Seen inside the running shed on the same date are Nos W22, W35, W17 and W14, at least three of which are devoid of their nameplates. *Bob Winkworth*

Below: Across the line from the running shed was the locomotive works. Here No W27 *Merstone* undergoes repair on 15 August 1965, having temporarily been parted from its crank-axle wheelset. In order to achieve this the bunker end of the locomotive will have been raised using the hoist — an effective (if, in wintertime, unpleasant) outside working environment. *John Bailey*

Right: A head-on view of No 31 *Chale* outside the works on 7 May 1960. It would seem that preparations were in hand to raise the front of the locomotive to replace the front pair of driving wheels. *John Bailey*

Far right: A final view of the front of the works in late-afternoon sunshine on 20 June 1959. There were six covered roads here, used for the repair and repainting of locomotives as well as carriages and wagons. Indeed, a newly outshopped coach, awaiting reapplication of its running numbers etc, can be seen on the right. On the ground is the cab roof of an 'O2', the remainder of the locomotive no doubt being within the works itself. The crane was hand-operated and can be seen to have had split-spoke wheels. *John Bailey*

Left: Bound for Ventnor, No W25 *Godshill* is seen on the climb to Smallbrook Junction on Saturday 9 June 1962. Visible this side of the overbridge is the gantry bearing the up distant signals for Ryde St Johns Road. The right-hand arm was in use only when the section between Smallbrook and Ryde St Johns was operated as two parallel single tracks, as per the winter timetable. *John Bailey*

Below left: Six coaches behind No 18 *Ningwood* approaching Smallbrook Junction with a limited-stop Ventnor service on 3 July 1965. The two distant arms referred to in the previous view are also just visible in the background. The 1-in-172 gradient at this point is apparent even from the photograph, and as limited-stop services did not call at the previous station of Ryde St Johns Road the locomotive crew could have some sort of run at the bank. *Tony Molyneaux*

Right: Another limited-stop Ventnor service, this time on 9 June 1962, in the hands of No W20 *Shanklin.* Possibly the smoke effect was by prior arrangement, as the locomotive appears to have steam to spare at this point. *John Bailey*

Below right: Approaching bunker-first from the opposite direction is No W21 *Sandown,* in charge of a limited-stop Ventnor–Ryde service on 9 June 1962. The train was recorded having passed Smallbrook Junction, and the crew can now take a short breather, as, aside from a short section emerging from Ryde Tunnel, it is downhill all the way to the Pier Head. In practice the timetable changed over the years, such that by 1964 the 'limited-stop' service in the up (Ventnor–Ryde) direction, as shown here, missed out only a single stop, at Brading. *John Bailey*

Left: Busy times at Smallbrook Junction on 20 August 1966. The crew of a Ryde service are giving up the miniature electric staff for the section from Brading, whilst in the background another 'O2' waits with what could well be another Ventnor-line service. It would appear that the up service was running late, as the timetable allowed for a 3min interval between up and down services at this point. A delay such as this was sufficient to cause a compound effect throughout the rest of the day's service on both the Ventnor and Cowes lines. *John Bailey*

Below left: A different signalman prepares to give up the staff to the crew of No W16 *Ventnor*, heading a limited-stop service towards its namesake on 3 July 1965. The driver appears to be scrutinising the photographer, possibly to checking that he is staying clear of the train, although he could also be monitoring the steam escaping from the Westinghouse pump. *Tony Molyneaux*

Right: The same location photographed from a different angle. This time, on 9 June 1962, it is No W26 *Whitwell* that is working south. In later years all locomotives faced south from Ryde, there being no turntables on the island; the facility to turn locomotives (and rolling stock) had disappeared with the closure of the Newport–Sandown route, which limitation must have led to increased wear on one side of the wheel flanges. *John Bailey*

Left: A final view of Smallbrook Junction, recorded in July 1965 and included because of the pose of the fireman — well, we assume he is the fireman. The train is a Cowes-line service, with No W17 *Seaview* in charge. Smallbrook Junction signalbox contained a 'knee' frame of 20 levers (including four spares) and was positioned so that the frame faced the Cowes line. *Tony Molyneaux*

Above: On the Saturday of August Bank Holiday weekend 1964 a somewhat grimy and tired-looking No W32 *Bonchurch* approaches the north end of Brading station with what the photographer recorded as a 'down fast'. However, if this is the case one of the headcode discs is missing, as there should be two (one below the chimney and one mounted centrally on the buffer-beam); perhaps the service that day was such that it was simply forgotten. The curvature of the line at this point is evident, whilst the gradient will have been in the train's favour for over a mile and will continue thus for a similar distance. The mountain of luggage being dealt with by the porters is impressive, whilst the three wagons are on the rather overgrown 185ft dock siding. Prior to 1953 the Bembridge branch had departed to the right, its course discernible from the curved hedgerow. *John Bailey*

Left: More luggage at Brading on 5 August 1964. Unfortunately on this occasion the locomotive details were not recorded, although the train was the 2.26pm departure for Ryde, where it was due to arrive at 2.41pm. Note that in this view one of the wooden coal wagons seen on the left has still to be emptied. *Tony Molyneaux*

Above: A view of the southern end of Brading station and, appropriately at what had, until 1953, been the junction for the Bembridge branch, No W33 *Bembridge*. Photographed on 5 August 1964, the locomotive was in charge of the 5.21pm stopping service to Ventnor, which was allowed a 1min stop here. Some idea of the

intensive service operated can be gauged from the fact that on summer weekdays there were no fewer than 18 down passenger trains calling at the station, plus a parcels train and one ECS working. *Tony Molyneaux*

Inset: A July 1962 photograph featuring the floral display on Brading's former down island platform, the far side of which was once used by Bembridge services. The signalbox stood behind the former branch loop, a clue to its position gained by the present of the point rodding. A few years earlier locomotives not required for the winter service would be stored at both Brading and Sandown. *John Bailey*

Left: South of Brading, the 1¾-mile section to Sandown was doubled by the Southern Railway in 1927. Contrasting with the stretch of line between Ryde St Johns and Smallbrook Junction, the double-track section here was worked as such throughout the year, with standard **SR** three-position block instruments. Seen just north of Sandown on 6 August 1964 is No W14 *Fishbourne* at the head of the 11.25am service from Ryde, calling at all stations and due at Ventnor at 12.12pm. *Tony Molyneaux*

Above: Passing the wherewithall for track re-laying, No W33 *Bembridge* is seen just north of Sandown (and some six miles south of Ryde) on 22 July 1961. From the north Sandown station was approached on an uphill gradient of 1 in 66, which meant that considerable skill was required to ensure that a train was brought to a stand at the required point. *John Bailey*

Above: The gradient of the final approach to Sandown station can be appreciated from this view of No W31 *Chale* bound for Ventnor on 22 July 1961. To the right is the goods yard, which at one time handled a considerable amount of coal traffic. *John Bailey*

Above right: Viewed from the south (Shanklin) end of the station, two passenger trains cross at Sandown on Saturday 25 July 1964. No W20 *Shanklin* (with patched side tank) is in charge of the southbound service, but unfortunately it is not possible to identify the locomotive of the Ryde-bound train. Sandown station marked the end of the double-track section, the following 1¾ miles to Shanklin being operated as a single line controlled by an electric train staff. According to the summer working timetable in force at the time of this photograph no trains were booked to cross at

Sandown, so presumably an earlier delay had resulted in adjustments to the service. *John Bailey*

Right: No W16 *Ventnor* in the process of running around its train at Sandown on an unrecorded date but probably a Summer Saturday. The 'limited-stop' headcode indicated to the signalman that this was an ECS working from Ryde not calling at intermediate stations. Sandown signalbox can be seen above the canopy of the island platform, the left side of which was once used by trains to Newport via Merstone. The locomotive is making its way south under the authority of a 'shunt ahead' signal (No 32 in the frame), installed as recently as June 1953; once this manœuvre has been completed the train will be shunted into the up platform to await departure. *Paul Bodkin*

ENTRANCE
TO
STATION

Left: A host of Southern Railway ephemera is visible in this photograph taken at the south end of Sandown station on 20 August 1966 as a filthy No W24 *Calbourne* calls with the 1.40pm from Ryde Pier Head. The 'shunt ahead' signal referred to in the previous caption is also visible. Passenger access between the platforms here was by means of a subway. *John Bailey*

Above: Having disembarked from the southbound train, passengers wait at the foot crossing as No W33 *Bembridge* pulls away from Sandown station on 5 August 1964. Unfortunately the railway's insistence that passengers enter and leave the station only via the main building on the down platform meant that the crossing was often busier than it might have been, and over the years there were several instances of 'near misses' between trains and pedestrians. *Tony Molyneaux*

Left: An interesting comparison in terms of cleanliness with the photograph on page 56. Here No W24 *Calbourne* is shown to be in excellent external condition, but this was 1961 — 22 May, to be exact — and perhaps at the start of the season time and resources were such as to permit regular cleaning. The locomotive is seen at Sandown at the head of a stopping train to Ryde. For now the platform appears deserted, but later in the year intending passengers will be standing perhaps six deep and even on occasions be queuing out across the station frontage and along the approach road. *Tony Molyneaux*

Below left: Beyond Sandown the single line continues to climb, the gradient being as severe as 1 in 80. There is then a brief respite, with an almost equally steep downhill section, before the line climbs again. Indeed, the gradient will now be against a down train as far as the entrance to Ventnor Tunnel, allied to which there are numerous sharp curves to contend with. Speed, then, was of little consequence, and instead it was often a question of slogging away with the regulator fully open and the reverser way down towards full gear for long periods. Such was probably the case here on 26 September 1964, as No W33 *Bembridge*, in charge of a Ventnor service, tackles the 1-in-80 section. *Tony Molyneaux*

Right: Near the same spot on 20 August 1966 a somewhat grimy and woebegone No W27 *Merstone* has charge of the 2.10pm Ryde–Ventnor, which, despite the lack of correct headcode discs, was scheduled as a limited-stop service. After the cessation of steam working at the end of December 1966 *Merstone* was one of eight members of the 'O2' class which ended their days at Newport, where they were stored for four months before being broken up; they could not be cut up at the platform where they had been stored, so ironically *Merstone* had to be steamed again for one last time to move the rusting locomotives to the breakers in the former Freshwater Yard. *John Bailey*

Left: In a scene dispelling the myth that the Isle of Wight is flat, No W28 *Ashey* is depicted against a cloudless sky in charge of the 10.45am ex Sandown, bound for Ventnor on 27 September 1964. *Tony Molyneaux*

Below left: No excuses for the inclusion of this unfortunately undated view — who could resist a photograph of a train passing through such a profusion of wild flowers? The locomotive is No W32 *Bonchurch*, seen near Lake with an afternoon stopping service bound for Ventnor. *Tony Molyneaux*

Right: Finally, before reaching Shanklin, we see No W22 *Brading* alongside Parsonage Road on its way south with a morning passenger working terminating at Shanklin. *Tony Molyneaux*

Above left: On a damp, grey day early in April 1961 No W14 *Fishbourne* enters the loop at the north end of Shanklin station with a train of empty coaching stock. To the right of the locomotive is the headshunt from the goods shed and yard, whilst behind can be seen the bracketed down home signal, placed on the right-hand side of the line to aid sighting. *John Bailey*

Left: In somewhat brighter conditions and viewed from the opposite side of the line, No W33 *Bembridge* leaves Shanklin station with the 11.56am northbound departure, which has crossed with the 11.56am south to Ventnor; the rear of the latter train is just visible at the platform. In the foreground (left) is the overgrown down siding, which despite its misaligned track displays evidence of recent use. *Tony Molyneaux*

Above: No W36 *Carisbrooke* runs around its train at Shanklin on 20 June 1959; the stock will have to be shunted into the up platform before the return working to Ryde. As at Sandown, the 'shunt ahead' arm under the starting signal was brought into use in the 1950s. Coaches were kept in sets wherever possible, set No 500 consisting of six vehicles (Nos 4136, 6356, 6362, 2416, 2452 and 4157). No W36 was one of the two last 'O2'-class locomotives to be sent to the Island, in April 1949; already nearly 58 years old even then, it would remain in service until June 1964, when it was condemned with defective cylinders and frames. *John Bailey*

Above: The next station south from Shanklin was Wroxall. Situated on a curve, it possessed only a single up siding, discounting the passing-loop used by passenger trains. In July 1965 the 3.45pm arrival (3.46pm departure) northbound is seen heading for Shanklin, Sandown, Brading and Ryde behind No W16 *Ventnor.* The large industrial building alongside was once a bacon factory. *Tony Molyneaux*

Right: Heading north from Ventnor, No W27 *Merstone* is seen at Wroxall *en route* for Ryde. The allotments on the opposite bank appear well cared for and may well have been tended by railway staff. The locomotive is coupled to set No 490, which at this time (1965/6) consisted of carriages 4148, 6351, 2414, 2446, 2451 and 4153. *Doug Hannah*

Above: Like any single-line crossing-point, Wroxall was characterised by long quiet periods punctuated by brief spells of bustling activity. Here, on 2 July 1965, No W21 *Sandown* waits to head south as No W31 *Chale* arrives from Ventnor. *Tony Molyneaux*

Right: Affording a view back through Wroxall station, this photograph shows No W35 *Freshwater* leaving for Ventnor with a light load on 2 July 1965. The station was on the 60-chain curve and on an uphill gradient for trains heading south. Northbound the line was relatively easy running, being mostly downhill almost as far as Brading. *Doug Hannah*

Left: No W21 *Sandown* and passengers leaving Wroxall for Ventnor on 2 July 1965; clearly this was a hot day, judging from the lowered windows in the front of the coach. The driver of No W21 was probably Eddie Prangnell, who in return for a donation to the SR's Woking Homes charity would often make the footplate available for those wishing to travel this way. *Tony Molyneaux*

Below left: Wroxall was just 1½ miles from the final station at Ventnor, half of this being on a rising gradient, the remainder sloping down through the 1,314yd Ventnor Tunnel to the terminus. The high-point, just prior to the tunnel, was also the summit of the entire line and was marked by Wroxall Manor Road bridge, from where this view was recorded of an up train bound for Wroxall and Ryde. *John Bailey*

Right: The site of Ventnor station — surely the most photogenic of all the stations on the line — once formed part of a chalk quarry hewn out of St Boniface Down and was itself 276ft above sea level. A daunting climb back, then, from the beach to the station, though the surrounding hillsides have some wonderful vantage-points for railway photography. No W20 *Shanklin* departs for Ryde on 5 September 1961. *Tony Molyneaux*

Another unusual view of Ventnor station, recorded from atop the tunnel mouth, from which vantage-point the complete site, with three platform faces fronting the two passenger lines, is visible. To the left is a loading dock and the goods shed, whilst to the right were more sidings and a number of coal staiths. Spare passenger vehicles were often kept in the sidings on the right. The photograph was taken on 18 April 1960. *John Bailey*

Right: The classic view at Ventnor. No W20 *Shanklin* emerges from the tunnel into daylight, with the roof of the signalbox just visible above the first coach, on 18 May 1959. *John Bailey*

Below right: With its two platform lines Ventnor could accommodate two passenger trains, as seen here on 18 May 1959. The line on the right, with a platform on either side, was known as No 1 road. The arriving train — behind No W31 *Chale* — will berth alongside, on No 2 road, although its passengers will have to wait until the Ryde service has departed before staff can put in place a number of wooden bridges to link the two platforms and so allow them to 'escape'. *John Bailey*

Above: The use of tank engines meant there was no need for a turntable at Ventnor (although years earlier a sector plate had been provided). Instead a locomotive was released and ran around its train by means of a hand-operated point at the south end of the site. This was also where the water column was situated, the railway having its own supply of water from a spring discovered within the tunnel at the time the line was built. This scene, recorded on 4 August 1964, features No W33 *Bembridge*. *Tony Molyneaux*

Right: Having replenished its tanks, No W32 *Bonchurch* runs back around its train at Ventnor on 18 April 1960. Slightly unusually the locomotive is using the loop siding to run round, whilst the platform loop appears slightly rusty; possibly there was a problem with the loop points on this occasion. *John Bailey*

Above: No W14 *Fishbourne* runs around its train on 5 September 1961. Within the tunnel were a series of illuminated signs and bells to assist in the various shunt moves; these were placed at intervals corresponding with the various lengths of train being shunted. The locomotive pit will be noted. *Tony Molyneaux*

Right: What is believed to be No W31 *Chale* ready to depart from Ventnor at the head of the then standard **BR** red-liveried branch-line stock in August 1956. After

the 1950s closure programme, 15 steam locomotives were still needed for the Summer Saturday service (although this number dropped to seven during the winter), the locomotives being required to run over 200 miles daily — not bad when one considers the longest journey was just over 14 miles between Ryde and Cowes. Unfortunately only 12 were still serviceable for the final summer of steam operation in 1966, which consequently saw a more restricted service compared with previous years. *Tony Molyneaux*

An unidentified 'O2' arrives at the Ventnor terminus on a hot July day in 1963. No fewer than 23 members of the class had appeared on the Isle of Wight at various dates between 1925 and 1949, but the closure in the 1950s of the various lines mentioned in the introduction reduced the need for locomotive stock, and four of the 'O2s' (Nos W15, W19, W23, and W34) were withdrawn in 1955/6.

The remainder were all active until December 1962, when No W25 succumbed; there followed a steady programme of withdrawals between 1964 and 1966, although two locomotives (Nos W24 and W31) were retained until March 1967 to assist with engineering works in connection with electrification. *Doug Hannah*

The platform at Ventnor station from the perspective of a passenger waiting to depart on a Ryde-bound train; visible in the distance is the tunnel mouth, with the signalbox immediately outside. Operation of the single line to Wroxall was by means of an electric train staff, which the crew will no doubt collect as they pass the signalbox. The photograph was taken on 29 August 1964. *John Bailey*

Left: Moving now into the final months and beyond, we see Sandown in the autumn of 1966. The conductor rail has been laid but is yet to be energised. Easily observed by the signalman from his lofty perch, a grimy and unidentifiable 'O2' waits with a train for Ventnor. For the present the station retains a somewhat faded green and cream livery. *Paul Bodkin*

Below left: Decay at Ventnor in 1968. It is two years since the last trains ran, the cost of maintaining the tunnel cited as the principal reason the modern railway did not continue all the way south. It will not be long before the scrap merchants arrive. *Paul Bodkin*

Right: Abandoned stock at Newport. After the decision to modernise only the Ryde–Shanklin section Newport became a collecting-point for all that was not required — locomotives, carriages and even redundant track. Today there is little sign of the town's once proud railway heritage, and instead the roads are ever more congested. *Paul Bodkin*

Below right: The melancholy site of former glory at Cowes. Where once trainloads of holidaymakers arrived and departed there is only silence, although the footbridge, at least, was rescued and now sees regular use at Alresford, on the Mid-Hants Railway. *Paul Bodkin*

Final fling for steam. Following the cessation of normal working at the end of 1966 Nos W24 *Calbourne* and W31 *Chale* were both retained to power the various works trains necessary in connection with electrification, to which end they remained at work (on paper, at least) until March 1967. *Calbourne* was recorded on a typical works train between Ryde Pier Head and Ryde Esplanade in the winter of 1966/7.